FAMOUS
FIGURES OF THE
CIVIL WAR ERA

Stephen A. Douglas

Champion of the Union

Colonial Leaders

Lord Baltimore
English Politician and Colonist

Benjamin Banneker
American Mathematician and Astronomer

Sir William Berkeley
Governor of Virginia

William Bradford
Governor of Plymouth Colony

Jonathan Edwards
Colonial Religious Leader

Benjamin Franklin
American Statesman, Scientist, and Writer

Anne Hutchinson
Religious Leader

Cotton Mather
Author, Clergyman, and Scholar

Increase Mather
Clergyman and Scholar

James Oglethorpe
Humanitarian and Soldier

William Penn
Founder of Democracy

Sir Walter Raleigh
English Explorer and Author

Caesar Rodney
American Patriot

John Smith
English Explorer and Colonist

Miles Standish
Plymouth Colony Leader

Peter Stuyvesant
Dutch Military Leader

George Whitefield
Clergyman and Scholar

Roger Williams
Founder of Rhode Island

John Winthrop
Politician and Statesman

John Peter Zenger
Free Press Advocate

Revolutionary War Leaders

John Adams
Second U.S. President

Samuel Adams
Patriot

Ethan Allen
Revolutionary Hero

Benedict Arnold
Traitor to the Cause

John Burgoyne
British General

George Rogers Clark
American General

Lord Cornwallis
British General

Thomas Gage
British General

King George III
English Monarch

Nathanael Greene
Military Leader

Nathan Hale
Revolutionary Hero

Alexander Hamilton
First U.S. Secretary of the Treasury

John Hancock
President of the Continental Congress

Patrick Henry
American Statesman and Speaker

William Howe
British General

John Jay
First Chief Justice of the Supreme Court

Thomas Jefferson
Author of the Declaration of Independence

John Paul Jones
Father of the U.S. Navy

Thaddeus Kosciuszko
Polish General and Patriot

Lafayette
French Freedom Fighter

James Madison
Father of the Constitution

Francis Marion
The Swamp Fox

James Monroe
American Statesman

Thomas Paine
Political Writer

Molly Pitcher
Heroine

Paul Revere
American Patriot

Betsy Ross
American Patriot

Baron Von Steuben
American General

George Washington
First U.S. President

Anthony Wayne
American General

Famous Figures of the Civil War Era

John Brown
Abolitionist

Jefferson Davis
Confederate President

Frederick Douglass
Abolitionist and Author

Stephen A. Douglas
Champion of the Union

David Farragut
Union Admiral

Ulysses S. Grant
Military Leader and President

Stonewall Jackson
Confederate General

Joseph E. Johnston
Confederate General

Robert E. Lee
Confederate General

Abraham Lincoln
Civil War President

George Gordon Meade
Union General

George McClellan
Union General

William Henry Seward
Senator and Statesman

Philip Sheridan
Union General

William Sherman
Union General

Edwin Stanton
Secretary of War

Harriet Beecher Stowe
Author of Uncle Tom's Cabin

James Ewell Brown Stuart
Confederate General

Sojourner Truth
Abolitionist, Suffragist, and Preacher

Harriet Tubman
Leader of the Underground Railroad

Stephen A. Douglas

Champion of the Union

Mike Bonner

Arthur M. Schlesinger, jr.
Senior Consulting Editor

Chelsea House Publishers

Philadelphia

CHELSEA HOUSE PUBLISHERS
Editor-in-Chief Sally Cheney
Director of Production Kim Shinners
Production Manager Pamela Loos
Art Director Sara Davis
Production Editor Diann Grasse

Staff for *STEPHEN A. DOUGLAS*
Editor Sally Cheney
Associate Art Director Takeshi Takahashi
Series Design Keith Trego
Layout by D&G Limited, LLC

The Chelsea House World Wide Web address is
http://www.chelseahouse.com

First Printing
1 3 5 7 9 8 6 4 2

Library of Congress Cataloging-in-Publication Data

Bonner, Mike, 1951-
    Stephen A. Douglas : champion of the Union / Mike Bonner.
        p. cm. — (Famous figures of the Civil War era)
    Includes bibliographical references and index.
    ISBN 0-7910-6402-6 (alk. paper) — ISBN 0-7910-6403-4 (pbk. :
alk. paper)
    1. Douglas, Stephen Arnold, 1813-1861—Juvenile literature. 2.
Legislators—United States—Biography—Juvenile literature. 3. Unit-
ed States. Congress. Senate—Biography—Juvenile literature. 4.
United States—Politics and government—1845-1861—Juvenile lit-
erature. [1. Douglas, Stephen Arnold, 1813-1861. 2. Legislators. 3.
United States—Politics and government—1845-1861.] I. Title. II.
Series.

E415.9.D73 B66 2001
973.6'8'092—dc21
[B]   2001028769

Publisher's Note: In Colonial, Revolutionary War, and Civil War Era
America, there were no standard rules for spelling, punctuation,
capitalization, or grammar. Some of the quotations that appear in
the Colonial Leaders, Revolutionary War Leaders, and Famous
Figures of the Civil War Era series come from original documents
and letters written during this time in history. Original quotations
reflect writing inconsistencies of the period.

Contents

Andrew Jackson fought against the British navy at the Battle of New Orleans during the War of 1812.

Green Mountain Boy

The citizens of Vermont practice the art of politics at traditional town meetings throughout the state. Everybody gets to voice their opinion at Vermont town meetings, on issues large and small.

One of the most skillful Vermont politicians was the 19th century U.S. Senator and presidential hopeful, Stephen A. Douglas. He is remembered in our century for the famous Lincoln-Douglas debates, which took place during the race for a seat in the Illinois Senate. Douglas also ran against Lincoln in his bid for the presidency. Words that echo to the present were spoken by Abraham Lincoln and Stephen Douglas in the course of those debates.

Stephen Arnold Douglas was born on April 23, 1813, in Brandon, Vermont, on a chilly spring day. He was named Stephen after his father, a respected town doctor. Dr. Douglas helped with the birth of his son. He had studied medicine at Middlebury College, 14 miles north of Brandon. The town of Brandon lies in a valley, surrounded by the peaks of the Green Mountain range.

As a newborn baby, Stephen lived in a small wood frame house with his family. The family included his mother, Sally Fisk Douglas, and his older sister Sarah.

Stephen was born at a time when the United States was fighting the War of 1812 against Great Britain. The original 13 colonies of the United States had previously fought the Revolutionary War for independence from Great Britain. Now a few decades later, Americans were fighting with Britain again. This time it was over freedom on the high seas. During Great Britain's war with France, the British navy captured American sailors and made them work on British ships. This happened so often that Americans became angry and declared war on Britain.

Stephen was only three months old when tragedy struck his family. While holding his young son in his arms, the 32-year-old Dr. Douglas suffered a stroke. He died instantly. His death left the family without a provider.

Sally Fisk Douglas took her children to live with her brother, Edward Fisk. A bachelor, Edward Fisk farmed the family estate in Arnold Hollow, a community about three miles from Brandon.

For the next 15 years, Stephen lived and worked on the farm. Along with his regular duties, Stephen learned woodworking. Another uncle, Jonathan Fisk, let Stephen use his tools and wood shop. During the winter months, when it was too cold to farm, Stephen went to school.

Stephen attended the Arnold District School, located on the turnpike to Brandon. He loved going to school because it freed him from farm chores. Although Stephen handled his responsibilities on the farm without complaint, going to school provided a special treat for him.

In school, Stephen did well at both math and Latin. They were hard subjects for most students. He had a good memory and a knack for understanding math problems. After school, he liked fishing and playing in the woods with his friends. Stephen was popular and made friends easily.

What people liked most about Stephen Douglas was his warmth and energy. He was always moving, always talking, always friendly. As he got older, Stephen grew more slowly than other boys. By the time he was an adult, he was only 5' 4" tall.

In later years, people took to calling him "The Little Giant." Though small, Stephen had a large head and piercing eyes. He was also smart and opinionated. When Stephen talked, people listened. Stephen hoped he might become a famous politician one day—maybe even president.

John Quincy Adams ran against Andrew Jackson and won the election to become the country's sixth president. He served from 1825 to 1829.

Stephen was interested in public affairs and world events. He liked reading about famous people in history. The deeds of men like Alexander the Great, Julius Caesar, and Napoleon Bonaparte thrilled him.

In 1824 the famous hero of the War of 1812, Andrew Jackson, ran for president. Stephen was 11 years old when Jackson first ran. He heard the local men talking about it, and he was keenly interested.

Many Vermont voters opposed Jackson. They preferred John Quincy Adams, Jackson's main opponent. But Stephen admired Andrew Jackson. He liked Jackson for being a war hero and for wanting to expand the United States to the Pacific Ocean. Stephen decided that he would be a Democrat, just like Jackson. When Jackson lost the election in 1824, Stephen was disappointed. But Jackson came back four years later and won the presidency.

Stephen soon mastered all there was to learn at the Arnold School. Other boys in Stephen's class were going on to Brandon Academy, a place that prepared boys for college. Stephen told his family that he wanted to do the same.

But life on the farm had changed. Stephen's Uncle Edward had gotten married. With a wife and baby, Uncle Edward told Stephen that he couldn't afford to send him to school in Brandon. Stephen decided that if he couldn't go to school, he would leave the farm. His mother tried to make him stay, but he refused.

Stephen walked 14 miles to the town of Middlebury, Vermont. He found an apprentice job right away with a cabinetmaker, Nahum Parker. Stephen sawed table legs, made washstands, and built frames for beds. Stephen enjoyed being out on his own, earning his own way. He also liked being away from the farm chores. Making things from wood was much more interesting.

The town of Middlebury also gave Stephen his first experience with politics. He attended town meetings in Middlebury, and the give-and-take of opinion at these meetings fascinated Stephen.

Many of Stephen's free hours were spent talking with other townspeople at the general store.

Ethan Allen is shown here engaged in the capture of Fort Ticonderoga in 1775.

People enjoyed his company and listened to what he said. Stephen took pleasure in the attention he received from political discussions.

Independent and self-reliant, Vermont citizens liked men who weren't afraid to fight. The famous Ethan Allen was from Vermont. During the Revolutionary War, Allen led his force of "Green Mountain Boys" in daring exploits. In 1775, Allen's troops won a great victory when they captured Fort Ticonderoga from the British. Even as a young man, Stephen felt proud of these Vermont traditions.

The election of 1828 pitted Andrew Jackson against President John Quincy Adams and two other candidates. Along with his friends, Stephen campaigned hard for Jackson. The supporters of Adams printed handbills with pictures of coffins on them. This was meant to remind voters of the five militia soldiers Jackson had executed for desertion

Stephen Douglas's political hero, President Andrew Jackson, faced a problem. The Federal government passed a tariff bill in 1832 that angered people in South Carolina. Tariffs are taxes on goods that come into a country from abroad. South Carolina wanted a low tariff so people could buy cheaply from Europe. Northerners wanted a high tariff to protect their industries. The people in South Carolina refused to pay.

A state convention declared the tariff "null, void, and no law." President Jackson threatened South Carolina with Federal troops. South Carolina Senator John C. Calhoun and Senator Henry Clay of Kentucky worked out a compromise deal on the tariff, and South Carolina repealed the nullification. The Civil War later settled the issue of nullification in favor of Federal authority.

Andrew Jackson was the seventh president of the United States, serving from 1829 to 1837.

during the War of 1812. Stephen and his friends tore down the handbills as fast as they appeared.

Different opinions about politics began to grow between Stephen and Nahum Parker, during the two years Stephen worked as Nahum's cabinetmaker. The older man did not support Andrew Jackson and said so. Mr. Parker also wanted Stephen to do "some menial services in the house." Stephen said he would do any woodwork, but he would not be a house servant. These differences led him to leave Parker's shop, and Stephen returned to Brandon. Stephen burned with ambition. He read every newspaper and book he could find about politics and history.

He found another wood shop job with Deacon Caleb Knowlton. Then, during the winter of 1829-30, Stephen became sick. The illness forced him to quit his job. Around the same time, his grandfather Benajah Douglas died, leaving some money to Stephen's mother. The inheritance allowed Stephen to finally enter Brandon Academy. But he only stayed there a year. There were changes at home while Stephen was attending Brandon. Stephen's sister

Sarah met and married a man named Julius Granger.

Julius's father, Gehazi Granger, was a wealthy widower. Gehazi met Stephen's mother Sally, who was still a young widow, and proposed marriage to her. She accepted. The two couples, Sarah and Julius as well as Gehazi and Sally, moved to the Granger estate in New York. They brought Stephen, now 17, along with them.

The family arranged for Stephen to attend Canandaigua Academy, an excellent boarding school near the estate. At Canandaigua, Stephen studied Latin and Greek under Professor Henry Howe, a Middlebury College graduate like Stephen's father. In class Stephen read ancient Roman authors like Sallust and Livy.

One day, Stephen became involved in a heated argument between two boys who wanted the same seat at the dinner table. Rather than fight, the boys selected two other boys to try their case before a board. Stephen was one of the boys chosen to speak. He was so persuasive that his friend won the dinner table seat.

Canandaigua Academy prepared students for careers in many fields, including schoolteacher. Stephen took school seriously. He studied hard and became active in the debate club. More than one Canandaigua Academy audience heard him defend President Jackson's policies.

In 1833, Stephen shifted his attention from classical studies to law. He decided to become an attorney as one step toward reaching his goal of a political career. But New York required four years of training before he could be granted a law license. Stephen knew his mother could not support him that long. Stephen learned from other students that becoming a lawyer was much easier in the west. Ambitious and restless, Stephen decided to strike out on his own. His mother gave him the money from his grandfather's estate, about $300. With this small amount of money in his pocket and big dreams, Stephen headed west.

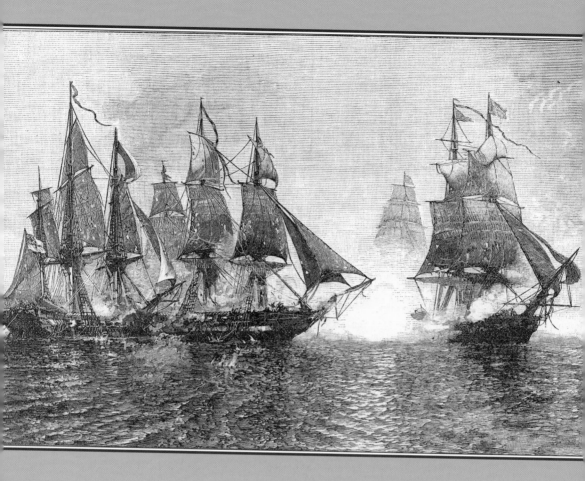

American and British battleships fought on Lake Erie in 1814. Stephen would later visit the area while he looked for a place to settle.

The Road To Illinois

Stephen Douglas was only 20 years old when he left home to seek success in the world. His first stop was Buffalo, New York. He visited landmarks like Niagara Falls and the battleground of Chippewa. From Buffalo, Stephen took a steamboat to Cleveland, Ohio. In Ohio, he came down with typhoid fever, a disease common to the swamps and wetlands surrounding Lake Erie. Stephen took several months to recover.

Even though he was running out of money, Stephen kept heading west. He was not sure what he was looking for, but he followed his instincts. Eventually, Stephen landed in the town of Jacksonville, Illinois.

In 1833, Jacksonville was a rough frontier settlement with less than 1,000 residents. As the seat of Morgan County, Jacksonville was home to the local courthouse. Outside of town, stands of virgin timber towered over fast-running creeks. In the flatlands, prairie grass grew waist high. Wolves and wildcats prowled in winter, and fish and deer were plentiful.

Stephen was down to his last 50 cents, and had to find a job. Stephen hiked from Jacksonville to Winchester because he heard that a teaching job was available there. The day after his arrival, a large crowd gathered in the town square for an estate auction. Before the sale could begin, someone had to be found to keep a record of the sales. The pay was $2 a day for three days. Stephen got the job.

The auction introduced Stephen to the people of Winchester. That helped when he was trying to enroll students in school. By December,

This advertisement for the abolition of slavery was made for the Antislavery Society, which was forming at the same time that Stephen became a lawyer. The poster shows African Americans going from freedom in their country to slavery in the United States. It also depicts the conflict between slavery and the right to liberty.

Stephen had enrolled 40 students, paying him $3 each for tuition.

While teaching school that winter, Stephen studied to become a lawyer. An attorney friend from Jacksonville, Murray McConnel, lent him a few law books, which he pored over at night. Home was a small room next to the pantry of the general store. After school, Stephen went to meetings of the town debate club, or **Lyceum**, as it was called.

At the Lyceum, Stephen participated in his first real debate. He defended Andrew Jackson against Josiah Lamborn, an experienced lawyer from Jacksonville. Holding his own against Lamborn, Stephen proved that he was well informed and a natural debater.

When spring arrived, Stephen felt he was ready to become a lawyer. A justice of the Illinois Supreme Court interviewed him briefly and said that he was ready for his law license.

Within six months of arriving in Illinois, Stephen had been admitted to the state **bar** in

1834. Now he could practice law anywhere in Illinois. Stephen closed his school and returned to Jacksonville to open an office.

Because he made friends easily, it wasn't long before Stephen developed useful contacts. Most newspapers in the 1830s were run by political parties. They often published stories about candidates and causes, using strong, colorful language.

Stephen won a friend after he wrote a flattering letter to S. S. Brooks, editor of the *Jacksonville News*, a paper supporting the Democrats. Stephen said he liked the stories Brooks ran in his paper.

Aside from politics, Stephen concentrated on his law practice. Although grasping complex legal issues would never be his strength, Stephen knew how to make speeches in front of juries.

A dispute between two other lawyers led to Stephen's first public office. The state's attorney for western Illinois was a man named John Hardin. A state legislator named John Wyatt detested Hardin. With the help of Stephen, Wyatt schemed to get Hardin out of his job. In February 1835 their plan succeeded.

The Illinois legislature selected Stephen as state's attorney for the First Judicial District. Although he was young to be a prosecutor, Stephen was enthusiastic and successful. In one noted case, the county name was misspelled on official court documents. The opposing attorney laughed and asked the judge to dismiss the case.

Stephen was angry and demanded to see proof of his mistake in writing. But nobody had a copy of the county record book on hand. An annoyed judge ordered the book to be brought in from a neighboring court. It took two days for the book to arrive. When they finally opened it, everyone (including Stephen) was shocked to find that he had spelled the name correctly.

Later, Stephen found out that he had indeed spelled the county name wrong. But then again, so had the government printer responsible for publishing the official book. Stephen said the incident taught him a lesson about handling opposition: "Admit nothing, and require my adversary to prove everything material to the success of his cause," Stephen said.

Stephen served as state's attorney for almost two years. He traveled the circuit court, meeting and making friends in each of the eight counties. He tried many types of cases and the juries he addressed did not forget him. In his free time, Stephen worked closely with his friend S. S. Brooks. Their goal was to strengthen the Democratic Party, first in Morgan County and later in the whole state.

As a strong supporter of Andrew Jackson's Democratic Party, Stephen worked to be a part of the political life of Illinois. He was convinced that his adopted state would be a major industrial center in the near future. He began buying land in a sleepy crossroads called Chicago and advised his brother-in-law, Julius Granger, to do the same. In a letter to Julius on May 24, 1835, Stephen wrote:

Stephen Douglas met fellow representative Abraham Lincoln in the Illinois House of Representatives. Douglas and Lincoln held different views on slavery. They would continue challenging each other in 1858 when both men ran for a seat in the U.S. Senate, leading to their famous Lincoln-Douglas debates.

"The most money is made here by speculating in Lands, for which this year presents the finest opportunities that have ever been afforded in this State."

Twenty years after arriving in Illinois, Stephen sold 100 acres in Cook County for $90,000. His 1856 gift of 10 acres of choice lakefront property gave the newly chartered University of Chicago its first permanent site.

For Stephen, though, making money was strictly a sideline. At the time of his entry into politics, there were two major political parties in the United States. Both were originally part of Thomas Jefferson's old Republican Party. After Jefferson left the presidency, his party split into the National Republicans and the Democratic Republicans. An earlier party, the Federalists, disappeared in 1816.

After a time, the National Republicans changed their name to the Whig Party. During the presidency of Andrew Jackson, the Democratic Republicans shortened their name to the Democratic Party. This was the party Stephen joined when he was old enough to vote.

Stephen and Brooks looked for ways to help Democrats in central Illinois. They heard that other states were using a new **convention system** to nominate candidates for elected office. Instead of letting everyone who was a Democrat run for office, Stephen thought the party should hold a convention to pick one person to run against the Whigs for each post. That person would be the "nominated" candidate.

Before the convention system was adopted, some people were elected who called themselves Democrats, but they did not support Jackson. Stephen and Brooks said they only wanted **"whole hog" Democrats** running for office in Morgan County.

As one of the promoters of the first Morgan County convention, Stephen benefited personally. He was nominated for a seat in the Illinois House of Representatives. Morgan County was entitled to send six house members to the state capital. Stephen was selected to head the local **ticket,** as the six Democrats were called. Leading the Whigs against the Democrats was John Hardin, the man Stephen had replaced as state's attorney.

When the election was over, the slate Stephen headed won five out of six Morgan County seats. Only Hardin was elected from the Whig Party.

In 1836 the legislature met in the capital of Vandalia soon after the election. The newly installed body met in a cold building, heated only here and there with wood stoves.

Almost immediately, Stephen became a leader. He helped pass bills to pay for a program of massive road and canal building. Also in favor of internal improvements was the Whig Abraham Lincoln, a second term representative from Sangamon County. Stephen liked the tall, gentle Lincoln. He was personally drawn to Lincoln and enjoyed his stories. He was also impressed by Lincoln's honesty and strength.

Lincoln did not return Stephen's admiration, telling friends that the 104 pound Stephen was "the least man I ever saw."

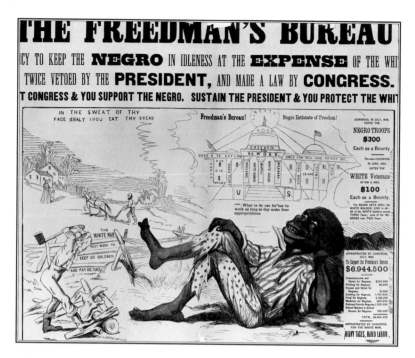

This broadside against the Freeman's Bureau was meant to inform whites that abolishing slavery would only benefit African Americans and have negative consequences for white men.

Lincoln and Stephen differed sharply in their opinions on issues unrelated to Illinois. Near the end of Stephen's first session, a bill was passed condemning abolitionists. People who opposed slavery were called abolitionists because they wanted to "abolish" the practice. Some abolitionists felt slavery ought to be abolished right away.

Although Illinois was a free state, many voters still believed that slavery was necessary. When the decision on the anti-abolitionist bill was taken, Stephen was one of 77 members supporting it. Lincoln was one of the six members opposing it.

The population of Illinois tripled between 1830 and 1840. After the 1837 legislative session ended, Stephen received an appointment from President Martin Van Buren to become federal register of lands in Springfield. The new job paid Stephen $3,000 per year, which would be useful while he planned his next political move. Already Stephen was thinking about running for Congress.

Martin Van Buren was committed to the concept of democracy and political action. He had a long and varied career in politics. Van Buren represented New York in the U.S. Senate and later served as governor of that state. He was appointed secretary of state by President Andrew Jackson and later was Jackson's vice president from 1833 to 1837.

Van Buren was the eighth president of the United States. He served from 1837 to 1841. As president, Van Buren continued to support the war that had started during the Jackson administration with the Seminole Indians.

Martin Van Buren served as the eighth president of the United States from 1837 to 1841. Van Buren appointed Stephen to the Land office as a reward for Stephen's support during the election.

3

Politics and
the Law

Martin Van Buren won the presidency in
1836 and followed his good friend
Andrew Jackson into office. Van Buren rewarded
Stephen in 1837 with the Land Office appointment for
his work on behalf of the Illinois Democratic Party.
Being Springfield Register of Lands was an important
job. As Americans of European descent pushed west-
ward, they bought land for farms, homes, and busi-
nesses from the Federal government. Stephen's job
was to handle the details of the sales.

Suddenly, the Panic of 1837 ended most of the sales
at the Land Office. The Whigs blamed Democratic

John Stuart was the well-known law partner of Abraham Lincoln. In 1838, Stephen lost the race against Stuart for a seat in the U.S. Congress by only 36 votes.

policies for the crisis. They said that Jackson had opposed a central bank and thereby weakened the economy. People who had supported Jackson, like Stephen and Van Buren, disagreed.

Whatever the cause, people had no money to buy land, and the country sank into an economic **depression**. Land sales fell from a high of $480,000 in 1836 to $68,835 in 1838. Stephen had fewer job duties and spent his extra time defending Van Buren.

The Land Office job profited Stephen in other ways. He was the first to know about valuable properties when they went on sale. The Springfield location also kept him in close contact with important Illinois politicians.

Stephen became a familiar figure on Springfield's main street. He cheerfully greeted everyone he met, shaking hands with the men and bowing to the women. Stephen liked people and thoroughly enjoyed talking to them. The pockets of his rumpled suits were always jammed with articles from Democratic newspapers, pamphlets, and brochures.

Stephen also attended every village social event, dancing with the young unmarried women. In the company of men, Stephen went to wrestling matches, shouting and cheering along with the crowd. He frequented the saloons where the men spent their free time, talking about politics. In 1838 women were not allowed to vote. Candidates did not have to appeal to women and generally ignored them. Politicians of the time were rough and sometimes crude in their speech and manners.

During the election of 1838, Stephen sought the U.S. Congressional seat from the Third District. It was a hard race. Stephen's Whig opponent was John T. Stuart, the law partner of Abraham Lincoln.

Stuart had a big advantage. The Panic of 1837 left many people broke and wondering how to survive. The land **speculators** had driven up the prices of many properties beyond their real value. The Whigs said things would get worse if Van Buren continued following Jackson's policies.

Stuart was expected to win the race easily. He was a well-known lawyer with solid credentials.

As a supporter of Stuart, Lincoln went all out against Stephen.

Lincoln wrote about the race to a friend, even making a comment about Stephen's height:

"We have adopted it as part of our policy here, to never speak of Stephen at all. Isn't that the best mode of treating so small a matter?"

The race grew closer as Stephen battled tirelessly against Stuart. Near the end of the campaign, the men spoke before a crowd in Springfield. Stephen used language that infuriated Stuart. Grabbing Stephen around the neck, Stuart shook him violently. Stephen fought back and somehow he got Stuart's hand in his mouth. The resulting bite mark scarred Stuart's thumb.

Although he was an **underdog,** Stephen conceded nothing. He kept on campaigning hard, causing Lincoln to worry for Stuart. Lincoln said "[I]f we relax an iota, we shall be beaten."

Over 35,000 voters cast ballots. Stephen lost by only 36 votes. Crushed, he considered taking

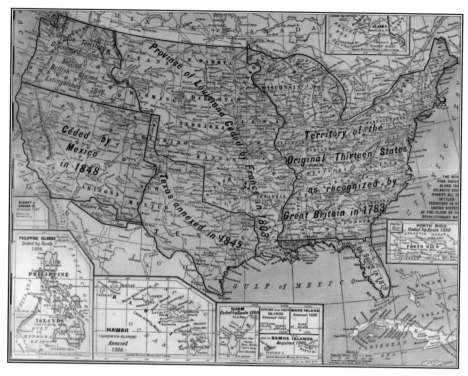

Many Americans believed in "Manifest Destiny." This was the concept that the United States was destined to reach from the Atlantic to the Pacific Ocean. This map shows how the United States looked in the 1800s. As the country grew, the question of whether or not new states would be free states, or allow slavery, became important.

the vote to court. But Stuart and Lincoln made it plain that they would question every single vote for Stephen if he did the same to them. Quietly, Stephen dropped his plans for a lawsuit.

Stephen went back to practicing law. He had quit his Land Office job to run for Congress and was nearly broke. When he made money, he spent it on politics or land purchases.

Life in Springfield, meanwhile, had many pleasant diversions. As a rising star in a political town, Stephen was the center of attention. For a while, he kept company with Mary Todd, who eventually married Lincoln. "I liked [Stephen] well enough," Mary said years later, "but that was all."

As he rose in prominence, Stephen gained entry to the highest councils of the Democratic Party. When asked about his ideas, Stephen spoke of expanding the United States to the Pacific Ocean.

The quickest way to do that was to build railroads, Stephen said. He wanted to conquer the Native Americans living out west and strip them of their lands. The ideas he formed at this time were best expressed during his later debates with Lincoln. During their first meeting in

Ottawa, Illinois, on August 21, 1858, Stephen said:

"I believe this government was made on a white basis. I believe it was made by white men for the benefit of white men and their posterity forever, and I am in favor of confining citizenship to white men, of European birth and descent, instead of conferring it on Negroes, Indians, and other inferior races."

After losing to Stuart, a new political opportunity soon came his way. The 1840 election placed the Illinois legislature solidly in Democratic hands. They named Stephen Illinois secretary of state, dismissing the Whig who held the post.

One month later, the Democrats enlarged the Supreme Court, from four members to nine. They wanted to make the court bigger so more Democrats could be justices.

Stephen was appointed to the Illinois Supreme Court, after only a month as secretary of state. The justices of the court were assigned districts from which they heard cases. Stephen received the western-most district, his home area at the time. Being a justice led him to be called "Judge Douglas" from that point forward, by friend and foe alike.

Stephen heard many cases during his service on the court. He wasn't afraid to take control of trouble-some situations, as when he intervened for Mormon founder Joseph Smith.

People in Illinois wanted the Mormons to leave the state. In 1844 the Mormon Prophet Joseph Smith had been charged with treason. To keep them safe, Smith and his brother Hyrum were jailed in Carthage, Illinois. But on June 27, 1844, a mob broke in and shot them to death.

Congressman Stephen Douglas advised his Mormon friends to leave Illinois. Brigham Young assumed the role of Mormon Prophet and migrated with his followers to Utah in 1847.

Calling themselves members of the Church of Jesus Christ of Latter Day Saints, the early Mormons were unpopular in Illinois. As the leader of a new and unusual sect, Smith was the object of much hatred. Smith taught the Mormons to call non-Mormons "Gentiles," and encouraged his followers to stick together. He also said Mormon men could marry several women and preached a type of Christianity that was foreign to most people.

Judge Douglas came to town to hear some charges that had been brought against Smith. Outside the court, a mob formed, calling for Smith to be hanged. Stephen said that no such thing was going to happen and looked to the local sheriff for support.

When the sheriff started wavering, Stephen dismissed him and appointed a new man in his place. Although he had no authority to pick a new sheriff, Stephen swore the man in and ordered him to form a posse to clear away the mob. Smith was saved.

Stephen's stint on the Illinois Supreme Court was brief. In 1843, he was elected to the U.S. Congress. The census of 1840 had given fast-growing Illinois four new congressional seats. His earlier race against Stuart had put Stephen at the forefront of the party. Stephen ran in the new Fifth Congressional District, opposed by Whig Orville Browning.

General Winfield Scott and his men entered Mexico City in 1847 and defeated Mexican troops in the last battle of the Mexican-American War. At the end of the war, the Treaty of Guadalupe Hidalgo set the southern boundary of Texas and gave New Mexico and California to the United States.

National issues like banking, tariffs, and proceeds from the sale of public lands dominated the race. Taking up the Democratic cry against a national bank, Stephen accused the Whigs of favoring rich people over poor people. He said that high

Whig tariffs hurt farmers and workers. His motto was the "greatest good to the greatest number."

Stephen won a seat in Congress. He served in the U.S. House of Representatives from 1843 to 1847. While Stephen was a congressman, the United States went to war with Mexico over the **annexation** of Texas.

Since winning its independence from Mexico in 1836, Texas had become independent, forming the Lone Star Republic. Both Texans and Americans wanted to bring Texas into the union as a full-fledged state.

Stephen believed in expansionism and was in favor of bringing Texas into the union. But Mexico objected, threatening war. Meanwhile, trouble with Britain started over the Oregon territory in the northwest. In both cases, Stephen favored gaining as much land for the United States as possible.

The slogan for Americans who wanted control of the Oregon territory was "Fifty-four Forty or Fight." That meant they wanted the northern boundary to reach into Canada, to the 54th **parallel**. They wanted the Rio Grande River as the southern national boundary.

An incident along the Rio Grande turned into war with Mexico. When it was over, not only did Texas belong to the United States so did California and almost everything else. On the Oregon issue, Britain and the United States settled on the 49th **parallel** as a permanent boundary.

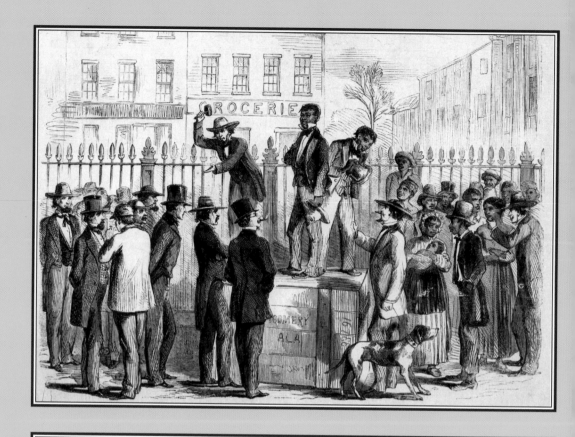

Men, women, and children were taken from Africa and brought to the United States. They were then sold to plantation owners in the South. Slaves worked for little or no money in the fields and homes of their owners, and they had no rights or freedoms. This arrangement benefited the plantation owners and was an important part of the Southern economy. Plantation owners could operate their farms with very few expenses.

Senator Douglas

In just 15 years, Stephen rose from schoolteacher to United States Senator. He served in the Senate from 1847 until 1861. Elected chairman of the Committee on Territories in the House of Representatives and later in the Senate, Stephen guided the admission of new states.

The toughest problem Stephen faced was the division between the North and the South over slavery. The conflict grew sharper with every passing year. Stephen tried everything he could think of to reduce sectional divisions. Democrats searched for strategies that would satisfy both parts of the country. It was a hard balance for leaders like Stephen to maintain.

Along with his election to the Senate came a new role as husband and father. In 1847, Stephen married Martha Martin, daughter of Robert Martin, a wealthy North Carolina planter. The couple had two sons, Robert Martin Stephen, born in 1849, and Stephen Jr., born in 1850.

In Congress, the politicians continued fighting over slavery. Stephen disliked slavery for the trouble it caused politically. When Martha's father offered him a Mississippi **plantation** with 140 slaves, Stephen refused the gift. He was concerned about the political consequences, he said. It would hurt a Northern leader to own slaves.

A year later, Stephen received the slave plantation when Robert Martin left it to his daughter in his will. If Stephen did not take it, the slaves would be sent to Africa, which they feared. Now Stephen had no choice but to manage the 2,500 acre plantation, despite criticism from his political enemies.

Stephen was pleased with the territory captured from Mexico after the war. The peace treaty, signed at Guadalupe Hidalgo, Mexico, provided new open space for American settlement. From the beginning of his career, Stephen had wanted the United States to stretch across the continent.

"I would make this an *ocean-bound republic*," he said in a January 6, 1846, speech to the Senate. He embraced **"Manifest Destiny,"** a popular folk belief that the United States had a God-given right to rule from the Atlantic to the Pacific. After defeating Mexico, the United States had made Manifest Destiny come true.

But the North and South could not agree on whether new states should be slave or free. The disagreement increased until 1850, when the two sides worked out an agreement known as the **Compromise** of 1850. Stephen was a key figure in its passage.

With Henry Clay, a Whig senator from Kentucky, Stephen helped write the five separate measures that together are called the Compromise of 1850. It preserved the union for another decade.

The first two measures provided for the abolition of the slave trade in the nation's capital and the admission of California as a free state. Slaves were legal property in Washington, but could no longer be sold in the city limits. Southerners considered this a great concession to the North.

An important Northern concession called for a new fugitive slave law. This promised Southerners nationwide help in returning runaway slaves.

The idea behind the Compromise of 1850 was to solve the conflict between the North and South. Senator Clay, legendary for his support of the union, was dying. Although a slave owner himself, Clay hated the practice. One former congressman who idolized Clay for his convictions was Abraham Lincoln.

But instead of improving relations between the North and the South, the Compromise caused more problems. Abolitionists resented the new fugitive slave law. Southerners believed that any restriction on slavery was a threat to their way of life.

The Whig senator from Kentucky, Henry Clay, wrote the Compromise of 1850 with Stephen Douglas.

Most people, however, were relieved that an agreement had been worked out. As a leader in the Compromise of 1850, Stephen won a national reputation. Newspapers in the North and South speculated about his presidential prospects. Two years later, the presidential race of 1852 gave Stephen a chance to see just how far he could go.

Two other Democratic candidates openly campaigned for president. Lewis Cass of Michigan and James Buchanan of Pennsylvania also wanted the nomination. Stephen planned to offer himself to the party as a **"dark horse"** candidate. That meant he would be ready in case Cass and Buchanan faltered. If elected at age 38, Stephen would have been the youngest president in history.

His friend George N. Sanders, editor of the *Democratic Review,* started attacking Stephen's opponents in print. Sanders felt that Democratic politicians needed to change their ways. Someone new had to bring "young blood, young ideas, and young hearts to the councils of the Republic," Sanders said. In the opinion of Sanders, Stephen was the man for the job. The language of the attacks was so harsh that

Stephen asked Sanders to stop. Sanders continued anyway.

These attacks damaged Stephen's reputation, as some voters thought that Stephen was behind the newspaper articles. At the June Democratic convention in Baltimore, Cass, Buchanan, and Stephen fought each other to a standstill. Other dark horse candidates put themselves forward as alternatives. One of the lesser known candidates, Franklin Pierce of New Hampshire, won the nomination on the ballot. Stephen was disappointed but assumed that he had another chance in 1856. Stephen did run for the presidency again in 1856, and once more he lost, this time to Buchanan.

His family suffered a devastating tragedy in 1853. Martha gave birth again, this time to a girl. Mother and daughter developed complications, and Martha died on January 19. One month later, the baby died. Knowledge of medicine was scant in the 1850s and people rarely lived to old age. Stephen and Martha had enjoyed a happy marriage and he grieved deeply.

As a remedy for his pain, Stephen took a tour of Europe. There he met emperors, financiers, journalists, politicians, even some English radicals. He discussed politics with everyone he met, learning first hand how Europeans saw America. When his trip came to an end, Stephen returned to politics with a renewed spirit. His goal, as always, was the presidency.

Back in the Senate, Stephen saw that the Compromise of 1850 wasn't working. Democrats began to consider the idea that voters in newly admitted states should have the right to decide whether or not their state would be free or a slave state. Stephen thought opening up the new territories to rapid settlement would naturally result in free states in the North and slave states in the South.

Determined to prevent further division over the issue, Stephen proposed the Kansas-Nebraska Act in 1854. This was an attempt to address the slavery issue with a doctrine called **"Popular Sovereignty."** It let new states decide the question of slavery during formation. States could then be admitted either as slave or free states. All Stephen wanted was for the nation to expand and grow strong. If a state allowed slaves it was no great concern to him.

Stephen was content to ignore the African-Americans, many of whom worked under the lash of cruel overseers. He believed that it was the right of the states to allow or restrict slavery as they saw fit. Popular sovereignty left the decision up to white citizens.

The Kansas-Nebraska Act was forced through Congress by Stephen with the help of President Pierce. Northerners who opposed slavery disliked Pierce. They branded him a **"doughface,"** which meant that he was from the North but was sympathetic to the South.

Passage of the Kansas-Nebraska Act gave Stephen the tool he thought would put the issue of slavery to rest. Once more the nation could go forward with territorial expansion.

Stephen pinned his hopes on popular sovereignty. But the first time the doctrine was tried, a

Franklin Pierce was president of the United States from 1853 to 1857, during which time the question of slavery in the Kansas-Missouri territory erupted into violence.

war broke out in Kansas. Proslavery and anti-slavery forces rushed into the territory, each determined to have the vote go their way. Proslavery forces burned and looted Lawrence,

Kansas. Led by abolitionist John Brown, antislavery forces answered by killing five slavery supporters in a brutal massacre. Newspapers dubbed the territory "Bleeding Kansas."

When it came time to adopt a constitution for Kansas, proslavery delegates met in the town of Lecompton. Though they were the majority in Kansas, "freesoilers," who wanted to keep the state free, were kept out by rigged elections. Resolutions passed at Lecompton assured legal slavery in the state.

Stephen had to oppose the Lecompton constitution.

The popular sovereignty notion promoted by Stephen received a hard test in Kansas. Once Kansas was cleared of Native Americans, white settlers moved in. Opening a new territory to slave owners angered Northern interests.

Proslavery men, known as "Border Ruffians," came in from Missouri. They terrorized free-soil settlers, burning farms and killing families. The settlers fought back with weapons supplied to them by abolitionist leaders like Henry Ward Beecher. The rifles were known as "Beecher Bibles," because they were sent to Kansas in wooden crates marked "Bibles." Beecher's sister, Harriet Beecher Stowe, wrote the famous antislavery novel, *Uncle Tom's Cabin*.

His stand angered many in the south. They said he was betraying them. Much as Stephen hoped to turn Popular Sovereignty to his advantage, it was a disaster.

If Stephen's stand on Lecompton angered Southerners, Northerners were just as angry about the possible spread of slavery. Many white workers and farmers resented the wealthy men who owned slaves.

As Northern opposition to slavery grew, Southerners began to become frightened. They demanded rigid slave codes and the strict enforcement of fugitive laws. Slave owners wanted no interference with their rights to control human property. The North and South moved farther apart.

A new political party, called the Republican Party, formed in the early 1850s, replacing the Whigs. The new party was composed of Northern merchants, farmers, skilled workers, businessmen, and professionals who believed that slavery was unjust. Republicans were leaders in their communities. The thought of slavery spreading to new states alarmed them deeply.

Republicans adopted a new national **platform** in 1856, calling for an end to the expansion of slavery. Joining the Republicans was a capable, thoughtful lawyer named Abraham Lincoln.

Stephen Douglas went into the 1856 Democratic Convention expecting to be nominated for president. Few Democrats supported Franklin Pierce, the sitting president. As author of the Kansas-Nebraska act, Stephen had a solid legislative record.

But Kansas-Nebraska had hurt Stephen as well as helped him. James Buchanan had been on a foreign mission when the bill came under fire. On the 17th ballot, Buchanan won the nomination.

Abraham Lincoln served as president from 1861 to 1865. He is shown here reading the Emancipation Proclamation to members of his Cabinet in September 1862. The final proclamation was issued on January 1, 1863, and freed slaves in the Confederate states that were in rebellion.

The Lincoln–
Douglas
Debates

Historians consider Stephen Douglas the toughest of Abraham Lincoln's political opponents. The two men battled each other for nearly 20 years. The most notable campaigns between them took place in 1858 and 1860.

The 1858 campaign got underway when Lincoln challenged Douglas for his Senate seat. The 1860 contest saw them in a fight for the presidency.

Two years before the 1858 campaign, Stephen married Washington socialite Adele Cutts. A grand-niece of First Lady Dolley Madison, Adele was beautiful and warm-hearted. She took responsibility

In 1861, Jefferson Davis was elected president of the Confederate States of America, which was made up of the proslavery Southern states. The Civil War between the North and South over slavery would soon begin.

for Stephen's young sons, Robert and Stephen. The boys had been moved around among relatives since their mother died. Adele raised them as if they were her own sons.

Adele's involvement with the children allowed Stephen to devote his energy to politics. Additional problems were putting new strains on his Popular Sovereignty plan. One challenge began when a slave named Dred Scott sued for his freedom. Scott said that because his master had taken him to places where slavery was illegal, Scott should be freed. The U.S. Supreme Court ruled that blacks were not citizens and therefore had no rights. Slave owners could take slaves into free territory as they saw fit.

Around the country, Republicans were outraged. They did not want slaves going into western territories. Whites were angry to think that slave labor might take away jobs from free workers. In Illinois, Abraham Lincoln practiced his arguments against the spread of slavery and waited for a chance to use them on Stephen.

Lincoln got his chance when the Republican Party of Illinois nominated him in 1858 to run for the Senate seat Stephen had held for 10 years.

Knowing that he could not win in 1858 without doing something dramatic, Lincoln challenged Stephen to a series of debates. Stephen believed he had nothing to gain from debating Lincoln but was too competitive to refuse. They agreed to seven debates, each to be staged at different towns around Illinois.

All seven debates followed a similar pattern. Douglas and Lincoln took turns making the opening remarks. The men knew their arguments and how to present them. For months they had been campaigning across Illinois, discussing the issues, especially slavery.

But these seven debates were special. At every one, Douglas and Lincoln exchanged remarks about slavery and freedom that will never be forgotten.

Many people turned out in the small towns to see and hear the two famous candidates. Everywhere enthusiastic crowds jostled to get the best spots in front. Well-dressed and well-groomed, Stephen traveled with Adele at his side. He rode from debate to debate in a private train car with a cannon in the rear. The cannon boomed to let people know Stephen was in town.

Lincoln traveled alone, on a free ticket supplied to him as a railroad lawyer. In his hat, he kept little slips of paper scrawled with notes for his speeches.

Their first debate at Ottawa in southern Illinois saw Stephen put forth his strongest effort. He accused Lincoln of favoring black people over white people. If Lincoln wanted to consider the black man his equal, he could do so. But Stephen did not believe black people were equal to white people.

Douglas attacked Lincoln's political party as "Black Republicans" and said Lincoln wanted to free the slaves. He said that Lincoln's views would lead to civil war.

Lincoln answered by saying that he did not want a civil war. But he stressed his belief that slavery was morally wrong. Lincoln said that perhaps African Americans were not the equal of whites in every way. But they *were* equal in their right to put food into their mouths that their own hands had earned. Slavery took that right away from them. Lincoln believed that slavery was a monstrous evil because it gave blacks no hope.

The rest of the debates followed a similar pattern. From August to October, Douglas and Lincoln debated, with additional speeches in between. As the campaign wore on, Lincoln grew more confident. At their second debate in Freeport, Lincoln caught Douglas in a trap. He asked if slavery could be kept out of a territory *before* it became a state. Stephen answered that it could.

Stephen's answer angered proslavery Democrats like Jefferson Davis and President Buchanan. His answer did not cost him votes in the Senate race, but it hurt him badly in 1860. By contrast, Lincoln's stirring moral arguments won him strong support around the country.

Abolitionist John Brown and his supporters planned to end slavery with violence and slave uprisings. They took over a Federal arsenal in Harpers Ferry, Virginia, but their plan failed. John Brown was convicted of treason and murder and hanged.

Douglas won the Senate race over Lincoln. Although the Republicans polled more votes,

John Brown had a daring plan to destroy slavery once and for all. He would do it by armed force.

On the morning of October 16, 1859, Brown led a troop of 18 men into the town of Harpers Ferry, Virginia. They captured the Federal arsenal and waited for the slaves of the South to join them. Instead, a company of U.S. Marines under Colonel Robert E. Lee killed 10 of Brown's men and put him in prison. Convicted of treason and murder, Brown was hanged on December 2, 1859.

holdover Democrats in the state legislature voted to keep Stephen in office. This was taken at a time when Senators were elected by a vote of the legislature, not by the people.

After saving his Senate seat, Stephen spent the next two years running for president. Things grew worse in 1859 when John Brown's band captured a Federal artillery warehouse in Harpers Ferry, Virginia. Brown planned to use the guns and ammunition there to start a slave revolt.

When the Democrats met in 1860 to nominate a candidate for president, Southerners were still angry at Stephen. He refused to be a "dough face" puppet of the slave interests. If slavery was excluded from some territories, Stephen saw nothing wrong with it, as long as Popular Sovereignty was followed.

The Southerners left the 1860 Democratic convention, splitting the party. The Republicans nominated Lincoln on the third ballot, mainly because he had been so effective in his Illinois debates against Stephen.

The Southern faction nominated another presidential candidate, John C. Breckinridge. Later, another Southern group put up a fourth candidate, John Bell. Stephen saw his chances for the presidency fade. Lincoln, the man Stephen had beaten in Illinois won the election of 1860.

After the election, **sectionalism** split the country apart just as it split the Democratic Party. Eleven Southern states seceded and formed their own country, which was called the Confederate States of America. The Civil War had begun.

The two tough races against Lincoln had weakened Stephen physically. It hurt that his doctrine of Popular Sovereignty had been exposed as a failure. After Lincoln took office, Stephen pledged his support in fighting the war. Only two kinds of Americans existed now, Stephen said, "patriots—or traitors."

In the end, Lincoln's ideas about halting slavery got him farther than Stephen's attempts to avoid the issue. A more progressive thinker had won.

Stephen Douglas wanted to expand the United States, no matter what. He did not care if expansion hurt the lives of human beings he considered inferior. Lincoln, on the other hand, also held views that many consider to be **racist**. Despite that, Lincoln saw the future clearly. Unlike Stephen, Lincoln was willing to say that slavery was wrong. Lincoln said, "If slavery is not wrong, nothing is wrong."

During most of his life, Stephen exceeded Lincoln in his successes. But Stephen avoided the hard questions and looked for easy solutions that would satisfy everyone. He won high office and enjoyed national fame. But his ideas failed to match Lincoln's grasp of what needed to be done about slavery.

When Stephen spoke in front of a crowd, the people loved to hear his thundering oratory. But afterward, when the show was over, they thought long and hard about the things Lincoln had said to them.

In June of 1861, Stephen died unexpectedly at the age of 48. A towering monument to him stands near the shores of Lake Michigan, in the city of Chicago.

GLOSSARY

abolitionists–opponents of slavery.

annexation–assuming political control of a new territory.

bar–an association of lawyers.

compromise–a decision that benefits all parties.

convention system–a method for picking candidates in an open meeting.

dark horse–a lesser known candidate for political office.

depression– an economically troubled time.

doughface–a Northern politician who favored the South.

expansionism–a political program designed to expand the nation.

lyceum–an association sponsoring public speakers.

Manifest Destiny–the belief that the United States should spread from the Atlantic to the Pacific Ocean.

parallel–an imaginary line sometimes used to set national boundaries.

plantation–a southern farm, typically worked by slaves.

platform–the program of a political party.

racist–a person who believes that one race is superior to another.

speculator–a dealer in lands or other property.

sectionalism–devotion to the way of life in a part of the country.

ticket–a group of party candidates.

underdog–the expected loser of a political campaign.

Whole Hog Democrat–a true supporter of Democratic Party principles.

CHRONOLOGY

1813	Stephen Arnold Douglas born April 23 in Brandon, Vermont; father dies a few month's after Stephen's birth.
1833	Settles in Illinois and opens a school.
1834	Admitted to Illinois bar.
1835	Elected district attorney.
1836	Elected to Illinois legislature.
1837	Appointed Register of Lands in Springfield, Illinois.
1838	Loses bid for a seat in Congress.
1840	Appointed Illinois Secretary of State.
1841	Becomes Justice of the Illinois Supreme Court.
1843	Elected to U.S. Congress.
1847	Elected to the United States Senate. Marries Martha Martin.
1850	Key figure in crafting Compromise of 1850.
1852	Runs for President. Defeated by Franklin Pierce.
1853	Martha dies in childbirth. Grieving, Stephen tours Europe.
1854	Wins passage of the Kansas-Nebraska Act. Champions the notion of "Popular Sovereignty."
1856	Runs for president second time; defeated by James Buchanan. Marries Adele Cutts.
1858	Debates slavery with Abraham Lincoln in election campaign. Defeats Lincoln for Senate seat in Illinois.
1860	Third presidential candidacy. Democratic Party splits and Lincoln is elected president.
1861	Dies in June 3 in Chicago.

CIVIL WAR TIME LINE ═══════════

1860   Abraham Lincoln is elected president of the United States on November 6. During the next few months, Southern states begin to break away from the Union.

1861   On April 12, the Confederates attack Fort Sumter, South Carolina, and the Civil War begins. Union forces are defeated in Virginia at the First Battle of Bull Run (First Manassas) on July 21 and withdraw to Washington, D.C.

1862   Robert E. Lee is placed in command of the main Confederate army in Virginia in June. Lee defeats the Army of the Potomac at the Second Battle of Bull Run (Second Manassas) in Virginia on August 29–30. On September 17, Union general George B. McClellan turns back Lee's first invasion of the North at Antietam Creek near Sharpsburg, Maryland. It is the bloodiest day of the war.

1863   On January 1, President Lincoln issues the Emancipation Proclamation, freeing slaves in Southern states. Between May 1–6, Lee wins an important victory at Chancellorsville, but key Southern commander Thomas J. "Stonewall" Jackson dies from wounds. In June, Union forces hold the city of Vicksburg, Mississippi, under siege. The people of Vicksburg surrender on July 4. Lee's second invasion of the North during July 1–3 is decisively turned back at Gettysburg, Pennsylvania.

1864   General Grant is made supreme Union commander on March 9. Following a series of costly battles, on June 19 Grant successfully encircles Lee's troops in Petersburg, Virginia. A siege of the town lasts nearly a year. Union general William Sherman captures Atlanta on September 2 and begins the "March to the Sea," a campaign of destruction across Georgia and South Carolina. On November 8, Abraham Lincoln wins reelection as president.

1865   On April 2, Petersburg, Virginia, falls to the Union. Lee attempts to reach Confederate forces in North Carolina but is gradually surrounded by Union troops. Lee surrenders to Grant on April 9 at Appomattox, Virginia, ending the war. Abraham Lincoln is assassinated by John Wilkes Booth on April 14.

FURTHER READING

Clayton, Nancy. Spellman, Susan. (Illustrator) *Strange but True Civil War Stories*. Los Angeles, CA: Lowell House, 1999.

Collier, Christopher. Collier, James Lincoln. Hispanic *America, Texas, and the Mexican War, 1835-50.* Salt Lake City, Utah: Benchmark Books, 1998.

Grabowski, John F. *Abraham Lincoln*. Philadelphia: Chelsea House Publishers, 2001.

Kummer, Patricia. *Kansas (One Nation)*, Mankato, MN: Capstone Press, 1998.

Moore, Kay. Matsick, Annie.(Illustrator) *If You Lived at the Time of the Civil War.* New York, NY: Scholastic Books, 1999.

Morin, Isobel. Politics American Style: *Political Parties in American History.* Brookfield, CT: Twenty First Century Books, 1999.

Newman, Shirlee P. *Slavery in the United States.* Danbury, CT: Franklin Watts, 2000.

INDEX

Note: **Boldface** numbers indicate illustrations; italic t indicates a table.

ABOUT THE AUTHOR

MIKE BONNER has had 12 books published, including *How to Become an Elected Official,* and *How A Bill Is Passed,* both from Chelsea House. Two of his books are on the sports card hobby–*Collecting Football Cards,* from Krause Publications and *Collecting Basketball Cards,* a Writer's Club Press title. Mike writes regularly for *Sports Collectors Digest*

PICTURE CREDITS